65 famous pieces of classical music

for solo piano

music masterpiece library

Table of Contents:

Corelli

Gavotte in F Op. 5 No. 10 1

Scarlatti

Sonata in A K 208 2

Sonata in G K 391 L 79 3

Sonata in D minor K 32 L 423 5

Sonata in C K 95 6

Handel

Gigue in D minor HWV 437 7

Bach

Prelude in C minor BWV 999 8

Prelude in C BWV 846 10

Minuet in G BWV 114 12

Invention No. 4 in D minor BWV 775 13

Invention No. 8 in C BWV 775 15

Invention No. 13 BWV 784 17

Clementi

Sonatina Op. 36 No. 1 19

Sonatina Op. 36 No. 2 20

Haydn

Minuet in C Hob XIX No. 5 22

Mozart

Sonata in C KV 545 23

Fantasie in D minor KV 397 27

Minuet in G KV 1 32

Minuet in F KV 2 33

Minuet in F KV 5 34

Minuet in C KV 6 35

Allegro in B flat KV 3 36

Rondo Alla Turka from Sonata K. 331 37

Beethoven

Sonatina in G major Anh. 5 No. 1 41
German Dance WoO 13 No. 9 42
Bagatelle Op. 119 No.1 43
Fur Elise WoO 59 45
Sonatina in F Anh. 5 No. 2 48
Rondo from Sonatina in F Anh. 5 No. 2 51
Menuet WoO 10 No. 2 53
Adagio Sostenuto from Moonlight Sonata No. 14 54
Adagio Cantabile from Sonata No. 8 Op. 13 58

Schubert

Moments Musicaux in F minor Op. 94 No. 3 61

Schumann

The Wild Horseman Op. 68 No. 8 63

Burgmiller

Tarantella Etude No. 20 64
Ballade Op. 100 No. 15 66
Arabesque Op. 100 No. 2 68

Mendelssohn Bartholdy

Song Without Words Op. 30 No. 6 69
Song Without Words Op. 30 No. 3 71
Song Without Words Op. 19 No. 6 72

Brahms

Intermezzo Op. 118 No. 2 74
Waltz Op. 39 No. 15 78

Tchaikovsky

The Sick Doll 79
The Doll's Funeral 80
The New Doll 81
Old French Song 82

Chopin

Nocturne Op. 20 83

Prelude in E Minor Op. 28 No. 4 86

Prelude in B Minor Op. 28 No. 6 87

Prelude in C Minor Op. 28 88

Waltz in A Minor Op. Posth. B. 150 89

Waltz in A Flat Op. 69 No. 1 91

Waltz in B minor Op. 69 No. 2 94

MacDowell

To A Wild Rose Op. 51 No. 1 97

Grieg

Elfin Dance Op. 12 No. 4 98

Waltz Op. 12 No. 2 100

Norwegian Melody 102

Arietta Op. 12 No. 1 104

Debussy

La Fille Aux Cheveux de Lin 105

Clair de Lune from Suite Bergamasque L. 75 107

Doll's Cake-walk from Children's Corner 112

Arabesque L. 66 No. 1 116

Joplin

Maple Leaf Rag 121

The Entertainer 124

Satie

Gnossienne No. 1 127

Gymnopedie No. 1 128

Gavotte in F
from: Sonata Op. 5 No 10

Arcangelo Corelli

Sonata in A Major
K 208

Domenico Scarlatti

Sonata in G Major

K 391 L 79

Domenico Scarlatti

Sonata in D Minor
Aria
K 32 L 423

Domenico Scarlatti

Sonata in C Major
K 95

Domenico Scarlatti

Gigue in D Minor
HWV 437, Suite No. 4

Georg Friedrich Händel

Prelude in C Minor
BWV 999

Johann Sebastian Bach

Prelude in C Major
BWV 846

Johann Sebastian Bach

Minuet in G Major
BWV 114

Johann Sebastian Bach

Invention No 4 in D Minor
BWV 775

Johann Sebastian Bach

Invention No. 8 in C Major
BWV 779

Johann Sebastian Bach

Invention No. 13
BWV 784
Johann Sebastian Bach

Sonatina
Op. 36 No. 1
1st Movement

Muzio Clementi

Sonatina
Op. 36 No. 2
1st Movement

Muzio Clementi

Minuet in C Major

Hob. XIX No. 5

Joseph Haydn

Sonata in C
KV 545

Wolfgang Amadeus Mozart

Fantasie in D Minor
KV 397
Wolfgang Amadeus Mozart

Minuet in G Major
KV 1

Wolfgang Amadeus Mozart

Minuet in F
KV 2
Wolfgang Amadeus Mozart

Minuet in F Major
KV 5

Wolfgang Amadeus Mozart

Minuet in C
KV 6

Wolfgang Amadeus Mozart

Allegro in B Flat Major
KV 3

Wolfgang Amadeus Mozart

Rondo Alla Turka
3rd Movement from Sonata K. 331
Turkish March

Wolfgang Amadeus Mozart

Sonatina in G major
Anh. 5 No. 1

Ludwig van Beethoven

German Dance
WoO 13 No. 9

Ludwig van Beethoven

Bagatelle
Op. 119 No. 1

Ludwig van Beethoven

Für Elise
WoO 59

Ludwig van Beethoven

Sonatina in F Major

Anh. 5 No. 2

Ludwig van Beethoven

Rondo

Sonatina in F Major, 2nd Movement

Ludwig van Beethoven

Menuet

WoO 10 No. 2

Ludwig van Beethoven

Moonlight Sonata
Sonata No. 14

Ludwig van Beethoven

Adagio Cantabile

Sonata No. 8 Op. 13 (pathetique), 2nd Movement

Ludwig van Beethoven

Moments Musicaux in F Minor
Op. 94 No. 3

Franz Peter Schubert

The Wild Horseman

Op. 68 No. 8

Robert Schumann

Allegro con brio

Tarantella
Étude No. 20

Friedrich Burgmüller

64

Ballade
Op. 100 No. 15

Friedrich Burgmüller

Arabesque
Op. 100 No. 2

Friedrich Burgmüller

Song Without Words

"Venetianisches Gondellied"
Op. 30 No. 6

Felix Mendelssohn Bartholdy

Song Without Words
Op. 30 No. 3

Felix Mendelssohn Bartholdy

Song Without Words
"Venetianisches Gondellied"
Op. 19 No. 6

Felix Mendelssohn Bartholdy

Intermezzo

Op. 118 No. 2

Johannes Brahms

Waltz
Op. 39 No. 15

Johannes Brahms

The Sick Doll
from *Children's Album*

Pyotr Ilyich Tchaikovsky

The Doll's Funreal
from *Children's Album*

Pyotr Ilyich Tchaikovsky

80

The New Doll
from *Children's Album*

Pyotr Ilyich Tchaikovsky

Old French Song
from *Children's Album* Op.39

Pyotr Ilyich Tchaikovsky

Nocturne
Op. 20

Frédéric Chopin

Lento con gran espressione

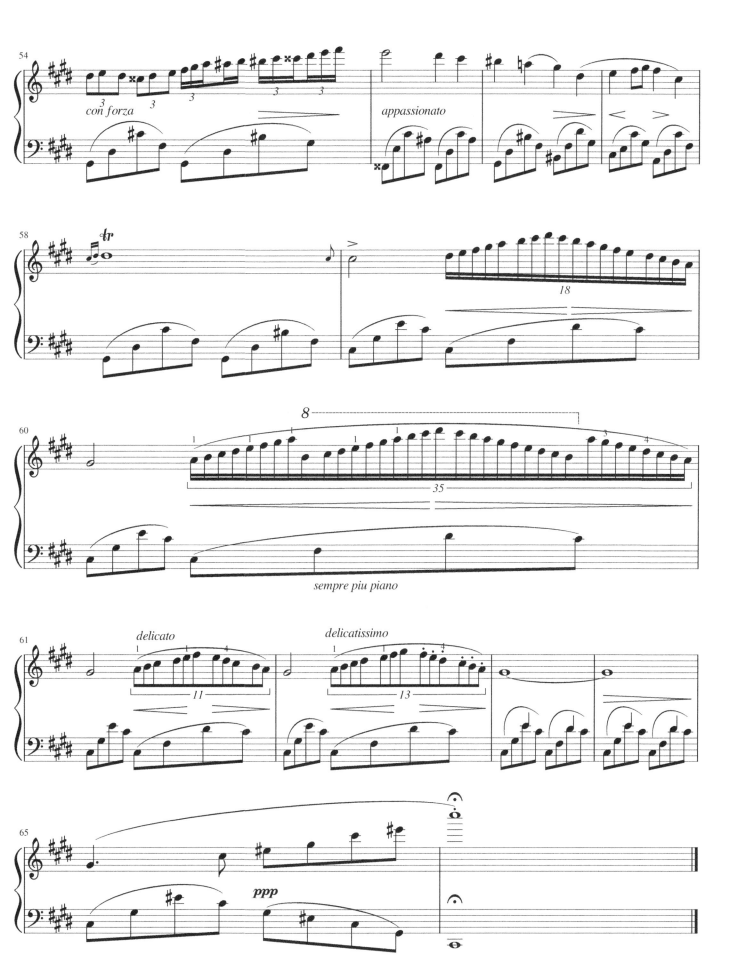

Prelude in E Minor
Op. 28 No. 4

Frédéric Chopin

Prelude in B Minor
Op. 28 No. 6

Frédéric Chopin

Prelude in C Minor
Op. 28 No. 20

Frédéric Chopin

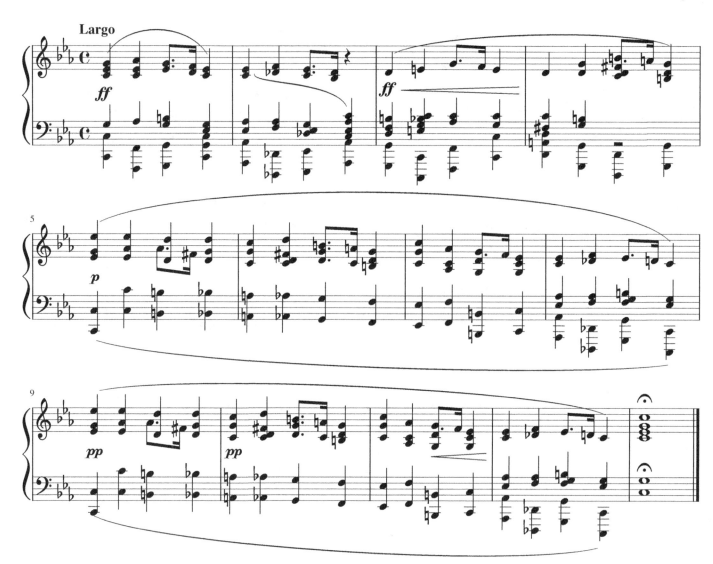

Waltz in A Minor
Op. Posth B 150

Frédéric Chopin

Waltz in A Flat Major
Op. 69 No. 1

Frédéric Chopin

Waltz in B Minor
Op. 69 No. 2

Frédéric Chopin

To a Wild Rose
Op. 51 No. 1

Edward MacDowell

Elfin Dance
Op. 12 No. 4

Edvard Grieg

Waltz

Op. 12 No. 2

Edvard Grieg

Norwegian Melody

Edvard Grieg

Arietta
Op. 12 No. 1

Edvard Grieg

La fille aux cheveux de lin

Claude Debussy

Clair de Lune
from *"Suite Bergamasque"* L. 75
3rd Movement

Claude Debussy

Andante très expressif

pp con sordina

Tempo rubato

pp

m.g.

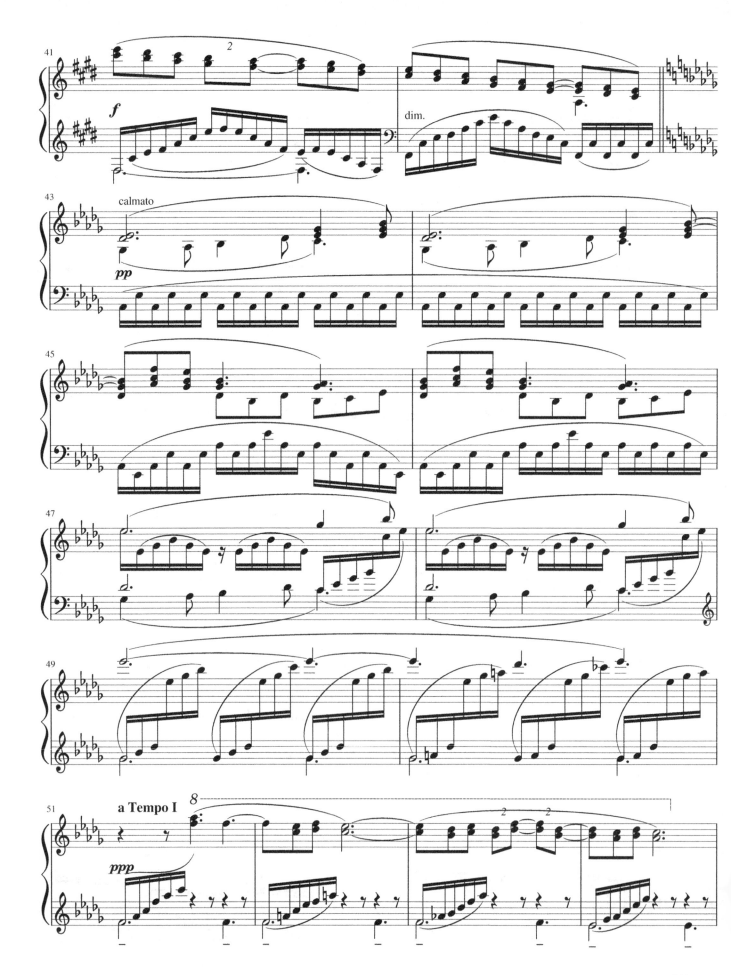

Doll's Cake-walk
from *Childrens Corner*

Claude Debussy

Arabesque
L. 66 No. 1

Claude Debussy

Maple Leaf Rag

Scott Joplin

Gnossienne
No. 1

Erik Satie

Gymnopedie
No. 1

Erik Satie

Made in United States
North Haven, CT
08 May 2025